The Pelica

The
Louisiana
Capitol

Tiered steps, massive portal, and imposing "Pioneer" statuary at left convey the grand scale on which the Louisiana capitol was conceived, designed, and constructed.

The Pelican Guide to

The Louisiana Capitol

Ellen Roy Jolly
James Calhoun

PELICAN PUBLISHING COMPANY
GRETNA 1980

Library of Congress Cataloging in Publication Data

Jolly, Ellen Roy.
     Pelican guide to the Louisiana Capitol.

     Includes index.
     1. Baton Rouge, La. State Capitol. 2. Art deco--
Louisiana--Baton Rouge. 3. Decoration and ornament,
Architectural--Louisiana--Baton Rouge. I. Calhoun,
James, 1935- joint author. II. Title.
III. Title: Guide to the Louisiana Capitol.
NA4413.B36J64   917.63'18   78-21239
ISBN: 0-88289-212-6 pbk.

Manufactured in the United States of America

Published by Pelican Publishing Company, Inc.
630 Burmaster Street, Gretna, Louisiana 70053

Contents

ACKNOWLEDGMENTS

The authors wish to thank the following who cheerfully shared a wonderful store of knowledge in the preparation of this volume: Mr. and Mrs. Solis Seiferth; Mrs. Leon Weiss; Mrs. Freddie Harris of the Louisiana Department of Culture, Recreation, and Tourism; H. Parrott Bacot, curator of the Anglo-American Art Museum at Louisiana State University; Mark Carleton, professor of history, Louisiana State University; William Clarke, professor of foreign languages, Louisiana State University; Frank Johnson of the Louisiana State University engineering faculty; Denise Landry and Evangeline Lynch of the Louisiana State University Library; Charlotte Melius, librarian, Louisiana State University Law Center; Lewis Nichols, Louisiana State University School of Geology; Senator Warren Davis Folkes; Dr. Bill Junkin; Mrs. James Monroe Smith, Jr.; Dr. Jack Jones; Henry L. Fuqua; and John Morony, Jr., Louisiana State University Museum of Natural Science.

PHOTO CREDITS

Mrs. Leon C. Weiss: pp. 14, 16, 90, 91; Solis Seiferth: 18, 19, 21-23, 25, 46-49, 50 (bottom), 51, 52, 56, 68, 70, 86 (bottom), 87 (bottom), 88, 92, 97, 100, 102-105, 109, 113 (bottom); Charles East: 26; Louisiana State Library: 12, 20; LSU Archives: 121-122; Louisiana Tourist Development Commission: 10, 41, 82, 84, 85 (bottom), 86 (top), 87, 106.

The Pelican Guide to

The Louisiana Capitol

Huey P. Long
1893-1935

Huey P. Long, one of the most dynamic personalities ever to flash across the American political scene, dominated Louisiana politics for seven years, serving as governor from 1928 to 1932 and as U.S. Senator from 1932 until he was shot to death in 1935. Ironically, he was mortally wounded in a still-unexplained melee inside the capitol, the magnificent structure he conceived, rallied public support for, and pushed to completion in only two years. Even today, more than four decades after his untimely death, his presence still looms large over the entire edifice.

Huey Pierce Long:
Father of the Capitol

Huey Pierce Long, fortieth governor of the state of Louisiana and later United States senator, was one of nine children born to Huey P. and Caledonia Long. (The Long children fell in and out of favor with each other over the years. Sometimes Long took care of them on the public payroll; sometimes they opposed him bitterly. His brother, Earl, was later to serve three terms as governor.) At the time of Huey's birth in 1893, the Long family lived in a comfortable four-room house built of logs in Winn Parish. Hard times were all around as he grew up: north Louisiana farmers scratching for a living, poky little towns, and few roads to travel to the great world beckoning beyond. Long's family was actually better off than most; but as a young husband he struggled to support himself and his family, and he never forgot the poor, the little people.

Huey did not graduate from the Shreveport high school he attended, but after traveling as a salesman he decided to study law. (He met pretty Rose McConnell again while selling shortening and married her.) He read law at Tulane University in New Orleans and then ran out of money. However, he persuaded the Louisiana Supreme Court to allow him to take a special examination. He was admitted to the bar after only eight months of

*The statue of Huey P. Long stands before the towering Louisiana
capitol, the nation's tallest state house. The flamboyant Long
conceived and pushed to completion the 34-story, 450-foot
building and in 1935 was fatally shot within it. A replica of the
capitol can be seen beneath Long's left hand.*

study—a remarkable feat at the age of twenty-one. Later, when Huey was governor, Loyola University of the South in New Orleans awarded him an honorary degree.

Long entered politics in a race for railroad commissioner in 1918. He had learned there was no minimum age limit, and he was only twenty-four. He won by 635 votes. In 1924 he became a candidate for governor. He lost in 1924, but was elected in 1928.

The stocky, auburn-haired man with the cleft chin who was sworn in as governor that day in Baton Rouge had championed the underdog in his law practice, had sought to break the limits on workmen's compensation set too low by the state, and was determined to defeat the oil interests in Louisiana. During his brief period in office he improved state institutions, added to the system of roads, built toll-free bridges, and gave free school books to both public and parochial school students. His unbridled tactics created many enemies. He believed the wealthy planters in southern Louisiana had run the government far too long. He did not understand the easygoing aristocrats who loved not classes and masses, but simply people. He was often vindictive: it was alleged that he had a telephone operator fired because she delayed connecting a call for him.

In 1929 Huey was impeached by the Louisiana House of Representatives and tried in the Senate. There were sixteen principal charges ranging from carrying a pistol to seeking to intimidate a publisher. For a time it looked as if Huey was beaten. He sent automobiles to various senators' houses and telephoned the lawmakers to come to Baton Rouge. Within a matter of hours, fifteen had arrived and were persuaded to sign a petition stating they would never approve impeachment proceedings—the celebrated "Round Robin." With this instrument Long managed to defeat the opposition and avoid conviction. During a subsequent session of the legislature in 1930 both houses passed a resolution dismissing the impeachment charges.

Long ran for the United States Senate in 1930 and won, but he refused to leave the state to take the oath of office, fearing

A huge portrait of Huey P. Long virtually covers the entrance way to the capitol as throngs gather on the steps for a "Share the Wealth Society" rally. Long was the leading exponent of wealth redistribution in the United States and campaigned on the platform "Every Man a King."

his lieutenant governor would assume control of the state. Two years passed before he went to Washington, where he burst upon the national scene, berated as usual by some and beloved by others. He was an early socialist, with his slogan borrowed from William Jennings Bryan, "Every Man a King." (His friend, Harvey Peltier, suggested this favorite saying as a title for Long's book which appeared in 1933.) He still managed to run Louisiana, returning often to stride down the aisles of the legislature, cajoling, coaxing, and arguing.

He died a young man—at the age of forty-two—fatally shot in the capitol he had built, leaving behind many plans for the future, as well as a wife and three children. His widow, Rose McConnell Long, served out his unexpired term in the U.S. Senate. His eighty-three-year-old father was too bereaved to go to the hospital that morning as Huey lay dying after the shooting. But it seemed as if the whole world came to his funeral: Acadian farmers, state employees, nationally known figures. The sunken garden in front of the capitol was filled with floral offerings from as far away as England.

Years later, in the homes of many of the rural poor, one could find pictures of Huey Pierce Long tacked above the fireplace. "He gave us bread," they said.

Taken on May 23, 1931, this photograph shows the rapid construction of the capitol, viewed from the south. Construction had begun less than six months before.

History of the Capitol

One of Huey P. Long's dreams was to build a state capitol. The old capitol, magnificently situated on a bluff overlooking the curving Mississippi, had been designed by the famous architect, James Dakin, and "testified to a whole generation's love of chivalry and romance." But the building had become crowded and old. Indeed, one of Long's opponents complained that the roof leaked over his desk in the House of Representatives.

In his book *Every Man a King* Long lists his first goal in the extra session of the legislature in 1930 as "a new state capitol at a cost of $5,000,000." Apparently Long's opponents spread the word among legislators that Long did not really want the bill authorizing the capitol to pass. After the votes had been cast, Long signaled Speaker of the House John B. Fournet not to announce the vote, since the board showed only sixty-five members voting for the capitol, less than the number required for passage. (Surprisingly, there was an electric voting machine in the House of Representatives at the time.) Representative Cheston Folkes of West Feliciana asked Long if he really wanted the bill passed. (Cheston Folkes, who with his son Warren Davis Folkes was to serve a total of more than sixty years in the legislature, was an independent. He had voted for one of the charges in the impeachment proceedings against Long in 1929. But he was always fair.) When Long whispered affirmatively, the representative from West Feliciana, a stronghold of the planter-aristocrats, cast his vote for the bill. This critical vote turned the tide; the bill eventually passed with seventy-three votes. Act No. 5, House Bill No. 9 authorizing the bond sale by J. E. McClanahan appeared on the statewide ballot on November 4, 1930, and carried over-whelmingly—108,761 to 7,761 votes.

Long selected the architects for the new building personally. While attending the dedication of a New Orleans furniture build-ing designed by the firm of Weiss, Dreyfous and Seiferth, Sen-ator Long mentioned to the man sitting next to him that he was

Workmen near completion of the steps and put the finishing touches on the front of the capitol in this photograph made on October 15, 1931. Note that the right corner panel of the frieze around the fifth floor has not yet been completed.

looking for an architectural firm to design the capitol building. The man was Leon Weiss, who said in effect: "Look no further. My firm would be happy to handle it." Solis Seiferth, the surviving member of the firm, recalls that work was begun the very next day. Some forty or fifty assistants were hired to help with the gigantic architectural task; in the amazing time of less than two years, the building was planned, designed, and erected.

A site for the structure was not hard to find in Baton Rouge. Louisiana State University had moved to its present location three miles to the south, and the old campus was not being fully used. Part of the land was occupied by a creamery owned by J. M. Cadwallader, who also taught dairy science at the university. Arrangements were made to provide land for the creamery in the northern part of Baton Rouge. The buildings were then torn down, and excavation was begun. Preservationists still regret that it was necessary to tear down the beautiful old home of the LSU president.

Long gave only two instructions to the architects: the building was to be a skyscraper, rather than the usual domed capitol, and it was to depict the history of the state. Architects, the contractor, artists, and craftsmen followed Huey's plan faithfully. The resulting edifice was a splendid, towering example of art deco architecture (sometimes called beaux arts modernism), abounding with historical detail. With thirty-four stories, it stands 450 feet high. For many years it was the tallest building in the South.

The contractor was the George A. Fuller Company, Inc. of Washington, D.C., which had built the Flatiron Building in New York and the Lincoln Memorial. The capitol was constructed of Alabama limestone. It was so large that for the first time since Reconstruction all of the offices of state government could be housed under one roof. The *Daily Journal of Commerce* stated proudly that features of the building included a "vacuum steam heating system, mechanical ventilation, and an ice water system serving the entire building."

America's foremost craftsmen joined with a small army of

Four views showing construction progress on July 3, August 1, August 8, and August 15, 1931. The magnificent building was completed in rapid fashion, requiring less than two and one-half years from the time architects were selected.

builders to erect a monument to Louisiana's past and a permanent symbol of its future. Because America was deep in the depression, world-renowned artists and sculptors were readily available. Their work makes the capitol a unique monument of art history. The building's craftsmen included Lee Lawrie, an apprentice of Augustus Saint-Gaudens; Lorado Taft, described as the dean of American sculptors; Adolph Alexander Weinman, designer of American coins and sculptor of the Soldiers and Sail-

Famed sculptor Lorado Taft directed much of the statuary work in the capitol. Here he poses with the central figure of "The Patriots" on the right in front of the capitol. The actual figure is in the foreground, with a plaster model in the background.

ors Monument in Baltimore; Ulric Ellerhusen, a pupil of Gutzon
Borglum; Jules Guerin, muralist for the Lincoln Memorial; and
the six Piccirilli brothers of New York. Lawrie was responsible
for the architrave and the temple. Taft executed *The Pioneers*

*The nearly completed capitol showing work still in progress
around the entrance. The wooden structure at the right of the
steps protects artists working on "The Patriots" from the
weather.*

An early plaster model of "The Pioneers," located at the left of the main steps. Marks on the photograph were made by the artists in the course of their work. The final sculpture differed somewhat from this working model, the cross being replaced by an open Bible.

and *The Patriots* on the capitol steps, while Weinman did the two relief panels by the portal and Governor Claiborne's statue. Ellerhusen was the sculptor of the frieze and the four statues on the tower and is seen at work as one of the figures in the frieze. Guerin painted the murals in Memorial Hall. The Piccirilli brothers cast the bronzework, and Attillio Piccirilli executed the statue of Governor Allen.

Louisiana sculptors were responsible for the twenty-two stone portraits of historical figures on the capitol exterior. These art-

Limestone heads for "The Dominations of Louisiana" on the sixth floor front balcony are completed and ready to be hoisted into place.

ists were Angela Gregory, Albert Rieker, Juanita Gonzales, John Lachin, and Rudolph Parducci. Miss Gregory and Miss Gonzales were associated with the famous Newcomb College Art Department, Louisiana's major contribution to art nouveau.

Throughout the project there was heavy pressure to complete the job quickly. In a letter to Taft on February 20, 1931, Weiss admonished the sculptor: "The present governor will relinquish his office very shortly after the contemplated completion of this building and has his heart set upon having the dedication of the building occur under his administration. . . . We feel no amount of effort should be spared to accord him the gratification of seeing the completion of this important portion of his program while yet in office as Governor of Louisiana."

The $5 million price tag on the magnificent structure may seem incredible today, but apparently the contractors and artists were all satisfied with their fees. Lee Lawrie was paid $43,900 for his contributions, including $1,200 each for the fifteen panels on the doorway. Lorado Taft received $31,000. Ulric Ellerhusen was paid $38,000, Weinman $45,000, and the Piccirilli brothers $40,875.

Workmen set into place the cornerstone at the southwest end of the capitol.

Among the citizens who expressed admiration for the imposing new structure were two Baton Rouge merchants. A friendly debate over the possible longevity of the capitol lead to a modest wager, recorded in a Louisiana newspaper during that period.

Heirs of J. D. Stotler or R. E. Collins, well-known local business men, if any exist in the year 2432 will, barring circumstances not presently taken into account, inherit $2,084,495,605.22 as a result of the filing of an unusual legal document here.

If on April Fool's day, 500 years from now, the new state capitol building is still standing, the heirs of J. D. Stotler will receive a 2 billion dollar fortune from the Louisiana National Bank. However, if it has been demolished, heirs of R. E. Collins will come into the money.

Mr. Stotler and Mr. Collins deposited $2.50 each with the Louisiana National Bank on April 1, 1932 to run for 500 years at four per cent interest compounded semi-annually. The money was accepted by Charles D. Reymond, vice-president of the bank, in a special deposit. The contract was drawn up by B. B. Taylor, local attorney, and is considered legal and binding.

The bet, placed on the durability of the new Louisiana capitol, was made over coffee cups when the men had a friendly argument concerning the life of the new building. The contract was signed in India ink, which is believed to be imperishable.

Stotler later released the bank from its obligation.

Capitol plaque.

A workman polishes the gigantic bronze chandelier before installation in Memorial Hall. Louisiana flora and fauna and replicas of the dominations of Louisiana are reproduced on it. The Piccirilli brothers fashioned the chandelier.

Aerial view of the capitol taken about 1935. Across the lake immediately behind the shaft of the capitol is Our Lady of the Lake Hospital where Huey Long died of a gunshot wound.

Capitol Steps and Exterior

Forty-nine granite steps, divided into four groups and flanked by imposing statues, lead the way to the entrance of the Louisiana state capitol. The thirteen original colonies make up the first group, marked by a circle of thirteen stars. The rest of the familiar forty-eight states follow with their dates of entrance into the Union. The Latin motto of the United States, *E Pluribus Unum* (one out of many), along with the names of the last two states admitted, Alaska (1958) and Hawaii (1959), is on the top step.

Monumental sculpture groups by Lorado Taft, towering on each side of the steps, immediately transmit the theme of the edifice—history captured in stone. To the left is *The Pioneers*; to the right, *The Patriots.* Explorers Hernando De Soto and Rene Robert Cavalier, Sieur de La Salle, are gathered around the Spirit of Adventure in *The Pioneers*, along with missionary priests, a frontiersman, a Spaniard, Frenchmen, and Indians. *The Patriots* portrays a knight standing over a coffin, with touching figures of mourners. Thus the portals are marked by those who explored and settled the state and those who sacrificed to keep it free.

The entrance itself is framed by the words of Robert Livingston, who in 1803 in France signed the Louisiana Purchase for

**The Louisiana State Capitol.
Diagram of the capitol showing
location of sculptural details.**

1. Stairway groups (Taft)
2. Portal (Lawrie)
3. Welfare reliefs (Weinman)
4. Historic frieze (Ellerhusen)
5. Foreign trade reliefs (Torrey)
6. Historic portraits (Gregory,
   Rieker, Gonzales, Lachin and
   Parducci)
7. Dominations of Louisiana (Lawrie)
8. Animals (Lawrie)
9. Crops, pelicans (Lawrie)
10. Corner figures: Law, Science, Art,
    Philosophy (Ellerhusen)
11. Spiritual temple (Lawrie)

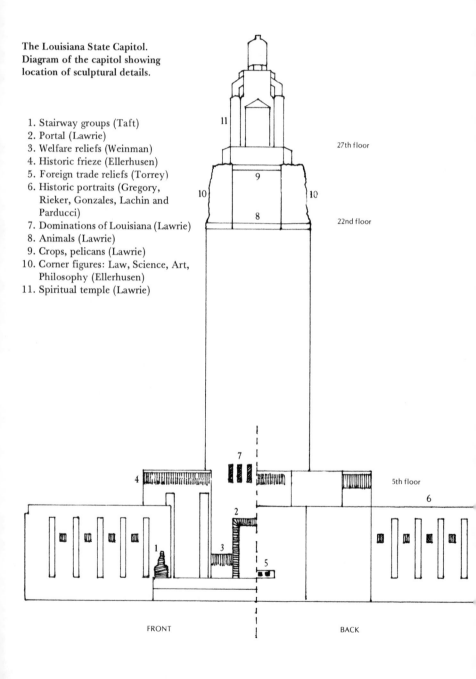

the United States. The left side reads: "We have lived long, but this is the noblest work of our whole lives. It will transform vast solitudes into thriving districts. The United States takes rank to-day among the first powers of the world." On the right side the inscription continues: "The instruments which we have just signed will cause no tears to be shed; they prepare ages of happiness for innumerable generations of human creatures."(—Robert R. Livingston, May 3, 1803/After the signing of the treaty purchasing Louisiana from France)

Adolph Weinman's two panels, on either side of the doorway beneath Livingston's inscriptions, show the Spirit of Liberty and Peace aiding the welfare of the people (at the right) and Government furthering the cause of the people (at the left). Reliefs around the main entrance show industries and natural resources of the state, with the motto *Union, Justice, Confidence.* (At the back of the capitol the motto has been rearranged for symmetry to *Union, Confidence, Justice.*) In a stylized and striking manner the various modes of production and employment are shown. Louisianians cut cane, pick cotton, fish, log, harvest, and build. In the models depicting transportation, note that smoke from the locomotive forms the waters beneath the riverboat.

The state seal with eagles beside it over the towering doorway symbolizes state and federal governments. Beneath the seal and the motto are men and women from education, science, the arts, and communications, and a row of robe-clad men with symbols of the law. (The architrave is by Lee Lawrie.) Soaring over them are representations of those who dwelled in and governed Louisiana at various times (from the left): Spain, the United States, the Confederacy, and France, flanked on both sides by an Indian. Interestingly, the Indians and France are represented by males; Spain, the United States, and the Confederacy are symbolized by statuesque women. All were the work of Lawrie.

Twenty-two profiles highlight the facade of the House and Senate wings and honor notables in Louisiana history. Five sculptors executed the twenty-two relief portraits with remarkable uniformity. These five sculptors were Angela Gregory, Al-

The architrave by Lee Lawrie is viewed in this photograph, the entrance being framed by the words of Robert Livingston when he signed the Louisiana Purchase in 1803. Adolph Weinman's relief panels are seen on either side.

bert Rieker, John Lachin, Rudolph Parducci, and Juanita Gonzales. From the left:

Edward Livingston (1764-1836), statesman who helped draft the Louisiana Civil Code; secretary of state under Andrew Jackson; brother of Robert Livingston, who signed the Louisiana Purchase.

William Charles Cole Claiborne (1775-1817), first governor of the state after its admission to the Union in 1812.

Jean Baptiste le Moyne, Sieur de Bienville (1680-1768), brother of Iberville, who accompanied him on many expeditions from the Gulf of Mexico into the mainland.

Rene Robert Cavalier, Sieur de La Salle (1643-1687), French explorer who arrived from Canada at the mouth of the Mississippi on April 7, 1682, and claimed the land for France, naming it Louisiana in honor of King Louis XIV.

Hernando de Soto (1496-1542), Spanish explorer who reached Florida in 1539, visited Louisiana, and proceeded as far as Arkansas; he was buried in the Mississippi River.

Pierre le Moyne, Sieur d'Iberville (1661-1706), Canadian explorer who passed the present site of the old state capitol in 1699, naming the place Baton Rouge (French for "red stick"). The name describes a cypress tree that, when laid bare of bark, was red.

Andrew Jackson (1767-1845), hero of the Battle of New Orleans in 1815 against the British; he later became the seventh president of the United States.

Henry Watkins Allen (1820-1866), brigadier general in the Confederate army and governor of Louisiana at the height of the War Between the States.

Edward Douglass White (1845-1921), Louisiana jurist who served as chief justice of the United States Supreme Court, 1910-1921.

Thomas Jefferson (1743-1826), third president of the United States; he authorized the purchase of Louisiana from Napoleon in 1803.

Judah P. Benjamin (1811-1884), statesman, philanthropist,

This massive bronze relief map of Louisiana is inlaid in the center of the Memorial Hall floor. Names of Louisiana's 64 parishes encircle the outline of the state, which depicts noteworthy products for which various areas of Louisiana are noted. The present railing was added later to protect the bronze from being worn down by the feet of the countless thousands who visit the capitol each year. Architect Solis Seiferth designed the map.

and United States senator from Louisiana.

Richard Taylor (1826-1879), son of Zachary Taylor and a Confederate general. His sister was the first wife of Jefferson Davis.

Francis T. Nicholls (1834-1912), Louisiana war hero who became governor in 1876; he lost both an arm and a foot in the Civil War.

Pierre Gustave Toutant Beauregard (1818-1893), Confederate general and adjutant general of the state.

Zachary Taylor (1784-1850), twelfth president of the United States; he left for his inauguration in Washington, D.C., from his home on the present state capitol grounds.

John McDonogh (1779-1850), philanthropist who established free schools in New Orleans, many of which still bear his name.

Julien Poydras (1740-1824), U.S. congressman and humanitarian who gave much of his fortune to Charity Hospital in New Orleans. He established dowries for needy young brides—dowries that are still awarded today in West Baton Rouge Parish.

Judah Touro (1775-1854), businessman and philanthropist who founded Touro Infirmary and a synagogue in New Orleans.

Paul Tulane (1801-1887), New Orleans merchant who founded Tulane University; he left the state during the Civil War to save his fortune and returned to leave it to his fellow citizens.

Louis Moreau Gottschalk (1829-1869), New Orleans native who gained international acclaim as a pianist and composer.

John James Audubon (1780-1851), world-renowned naturalist and painter; he tutored at Oakley Plantation near St. Francisville and painted the birds he found in the nearby Feliciana woods, which he called his "Happy Land."

Charles Gayarre (1805-1898), first serious historian of Louisiana and author of the four-volume *History of Louisiana*, which is still in print.

The famous capitol steps with the names of each state and its date of entry into the Union are seen from above. Visitors invariably look for the step with their state's name as they climb to Memorial Hall.

The cornerstone on the southwest wing was laid on May 7, 1931. It contains documents related to the structure, as well as photographs and names of state officials and those instrumental in the building's construction. *We live for those we love* is inscribed above the state seal.

One eye-catching feature of the exterior is the historial frieze almost encircling the building at the fifth-floor level. With slight modifications, this frieze is repeated high on the wall inside Memorial Hall. Rich in detail, the frieze depicts a wide range of scenes from the earliest explorations through World War I. The frieze concludes showing the state involved in pacific pursuits and pleasures and figures of jurists from Louisiana and elsewhere. Finally, the capitol architects are shown discussing plans with Huey P. Long. The whole of the frieze is a dramatic lesson in

The beauty and profuse symbolism of the capitol are evident in this view taken shortly after it was completed. The building was dedicated at the inauguration of Governor Oscar K. Allen on May 16, 1932.

state history, executed with vigor and accuracy by Ulric Ellerhusen.

The left front section is to be viewed right to left, starting with
Robert de La Salle's discovery of the mouth of the Mississippi
in 1682. The scene to the left depicts explorers Iberville and
Bienville. Next are a pioneer building, a log cabin and Antoine
Crozat, the first man to settle the region for economic purposes.
Bienville stands close by with Adrien de Pauger, the engineer who
planned the city of New Orleans in 1721. The romance of the
casket girls is portrayed next, showing young girls sent from

*"The Patriots" is also credited to Lorado Taft, and shows a
knight in armor above the coffin of a fallen hero with a lamenting
aged couple and a grieving man with hat removed. In the background above are four of the 22 portraits of noted Louisianians
on the capitol's exterior. Five sculptors collaborated on the
portraits.*

France to marry the settlers. They appear before the Ursuline nuns with their trunks, or caskets (in French, cassettes). Models for the two orphans with the nuns were children of the capitol architects—Solis Seiferth, Jr. and Carol Dreyfous.

Continuing to the left, Bienville appears again as royal French governor of Louisiana, followed by Bernardo de Galvez, a Spanish governor. The transfer of Louisiana from Spain to France is then commemorated as Governor Jean Manuel de Salcedo gives the keys of New Orleans to the French prefect, Pierre Clement de Laussat. James Monroe and Robert Livingston conclude the

"The Patriots" includes a group of men and women with symbolic wreath, citizens of Louisiana in mourning.

"The Pioneers" sculpture by Taft shows those who explored and settled the state around an allegorical figure called "The Spirit of Adventure."

Louisiana Purchase in the next scene (the price was $15,000,000), with Charles Maurice de Talleyrand-Perigord representing France. Around the corner on the west wall American governor William C. C. Claiborne, in charge of civil affairs in the colony at the time, presides over a flag-raising ceremony.

The east front section begins with the burial of De Soto in the Mississippi River. One hundred years later in 1663 Father Jacques Marquette and Louis Joliet came down the river as far as the Arkansas River. Here they receive a peace pipe from an Indian chief. The red stick is shown next as Iberville talks with the Houmas Indians. Since carved totem poles were not known to exist this far south, it is believed that the "baton rouge" was a cypress tree, or possibly a pole stained red with the blood of

In this side view of "The Pioneers" may be seen a buckskin-clad backwoodsman, a Spanish conquistador, an Indian, and a Franciscan friar, all contributors to Louisiana's colorful history.

animals and fish. To the right, Bienville receives a letter from the Bayougoula Indian chief. The faithful Indians had kept this letter, written by Henri de Tonti fourteen years earlier, and it proved that the river had been claimed for France by La Salle. The tranquility reflected in these scenes was destroyed in 1729 by the Natchez Massacre when the Natchez Indians revolted against the tyrannical commandant at Fort Rosalie. The Natchez nation was soon destroyed in retaliation. Chief Great Sun is portrayed here.

The expulsion of the Acadians from Nova Scotia by the British is recalled in the next scene as the Acadians (later called Cajuns) arrive in Louisiana. Betty Weiss is shown with the Acadian family, while Celia Seiferth and Felix John Dreyfous play near the

"The Dominations of Louisiana"—representing nations and peoples who once governed the state—are pictured above the entrance: Indians at each end, Spain, the United States, the Confederacy, and France.

skirts of the mammy. Once again a peaceful interlude is juxtaposed with violence: five men who rebelled against Governor Antonio Ulloa were sentenced to death before a firing squad by General Alejandro O'Reilly in 1768. The Battle of New Orleans (fought and won after the War of 1812 was officially over) is shown in detail next. Pirate Jean Lafitte offers his services in the war to Governor Claiborne, and Andrew Jackson (in a pose similar to that in Jackson Square in New Orleans) leads the charge against the British at Chalmette.

On the west wall, the frieze shows Louisiana at war, symbolized by a woman with a sword, accompanied by a pelican. The Mexican War, the Civil War, the Spanish-American War, and World War I are all realistically recaptured in a few figures: General Zachary Taylor, hero of the Mexican War; the Washington Artillery of New Orleans and the Confederate infantry (under General P. G. T. Beauregard) in the Civil War; Colonel Theo-

The cornerstone bears the statement "We Live For Those We Love." Also included are the state seal and the state motto Union, Confidence, Justice. *The Louisiana territory was purchased in 1803.*

dore Roosevelt in the Spanish-American War; and Louisiana's
John A. LeJeune, hero of World War I and later commandant of
the marines.

The east wall frieze is devoted to Louisiana at peace. The
scene includes a kneeling woman with a dove of peace, looking
over her shoulder at countrymen picking cotton, cutting sugarcane, and plowing ground for truck farming. Trapping and fishing in the marsh blend into the loading of ships at the New
Orleans docks. Mardi Gras provides a holiday for the workers.
The woman representing peace is one of the few allegorical
figures used in the artwork, since the architects felt that the
history of Louisiana was so colorful that allegorical figures were
not necessary.

The state motto, Union, Justice, Confidence, *is carved into the
north side of the capitol, but the words are transposed for purposes of symmetry.*

Delicate bronzework in the windows of the legislative chambers depict magnolias, the state flower. Portraits of Governor Francis T. Nicholls and General P. G. T. Beauregard are part of the ornamental frieze encircling the building.

Around the corner on the north wall are other facets of the
state: education, historiography, natural science, engineering,
fine arts, and architecture. John McDonogh is honored by New

*A bronze plaque at the left of the capitol entrance is dedicated
to the old state house. The old capitol is located several blocks
south of the new building.*

Orleans school children; Charles Gayarre writes his history; John James Audubon paints a flight of birds. A levee building scene comes next, particularly appropriate because the capitol is set near just such a levee. Sculptor Ulric Ellerhusen pictures him-

Bronze plaque at the right inside the foyer of the main portal commemorates the magnificent capitol.

self at work on the figure of Art for the tower, and Governor Long appears with Leon Weiss, Julius Dreyfous and Solis Seiferth, the architects. Weiss, the senior partner, stands with Long, while Dreyfous and Seiferth study the blueprint.

The evolution of Louisiana law is the theme of the relief sculpture on the center of the north wall. Lawgivers Hammurabi, Ikhnaton, Solon, and Justinian (from the left), and Moses, Solomon, Julius Caesar, and Charlemagne mingle here at each end of the band. In the middle, Edward Livingston, Louis Moreau Lislet, and Pierre Derbigny draft the Louisiana Code in 1824, with Napoleon and a French lawyer preparing the Code Napoleon. (Louisiana is noted for its Napoleonic Code. Napoleon believed that he would be remembered for this long after his victories in bat-

Intricate bronzework above the main entrance depicts the brown pelican, Louisiana's official state bird.

Under the supervision of Lorado Taft, artists meticulously sculpt the statuary groups flanking the capitol entrance.

Four allegories representing foreign trade adorn the north balcony (from left): the Orient, Latin America, the West Indies, and Europe.

Fifth floor frieze, "Louisiana at Peace," east wall (from left): Agriculture, Trapping, Fishing, Shipping.

tle would be forgotten.) General O'Reilly represents Spanish law. Symbols of justice center this series: scales and fasces are shown on a throne flanked by pelicans. To the right, Bienville, with a Negro slave, presents the Black Code of 1724, which protected the slaves but prevented their assembling or carrying weapons. The United States Constitution, drafted in 1787, holds the attention of Washington, Jefferson, Franklin, Hamilton, and Madison as they gather around a table.

Immediately inside the glass entrance doors on each side is a plaque dedicated to the two capitols, called in the old manner "the State House." The Old State Capitol was erected in 1847. Note that the name of the famous architect who built it, J. H. Dakin, is misspelled in bronze. To the right is a similar plaque stating that the present state house was erected A.D. 1931 and dedicated on May 16, 1932, at the inauguration of Governor Oscar K. Allen.

Another view of "Louisiana at Peace" frieze.

Fifth floor frieze, "Louisiana Law," north wall. The figure at left represents the Code of Louis XIV, while the figure on the right symbolizes the Code of Hammurabi. Gathered around the table are five figures drafting the United States Constitution.

Plaster model of the Battle of New Orleans, corner of east wall. General Andrew Jackson, mounted on a rearing horse, leads his men to victory.

Fifth floor frieze, west wall: Louisiana's American governor William C. C. Claiborne directs the flag-raising ceremony marking the transfer of Louisiana from France to the United States in 1803.

This fifth floor frieze on the west wall shows a bitter chapter in the state's history, the Civil War.

Governors Iberville and Bienville flank a scene depicting the arrival in New Orleans of the casket girls. Fifth floor, front wall.

The revelry of Mardi Gras in New Orleans, east wall.

One of the dominant attractions in Memorial Hall is the bronze relief map of the state shown here at center (see also page 32). To the left are the bronze elevator doors bearing portraits of past governors of Louisiana. On the balcony above them are the flags that have flown over Louisiana and a likeness of Huey Long.

Memorial Hall

Solemn and imposing stands Memorial Hall. Here one is reminded of Louisiana's past by the frieze, the statues, the murals, and the doors. Even the ceiling and the chandeliers have as their theme earlier days of the state. Dimensions of the hall are on a grand scale. It measures 120 feet long by 40 feet wide by 37 feet high. Memorial Hall has appropriately been called Louisiana's Hall of Fame.

The four statues in Memorial Hall were executed by different sculptors: Bienville by Albert Rieker, William C. C. Claiborne by Adolph A. Weinman, Henry Watkins Allen by Attillio Piccirilli, and Francis T. Nicholls by Isadore Konti. Jean Baptiste le Moyne, Sieur de Bienville, was one of fourteen children of a remarkable Canadian family. Three of the sons were governors of cities or provinces, and one of the daughters married a governor. The twenty-one-year-old Bienville became governor of Louisiana in 1701, served again in 1718, and returned to Louisiana in 1733 to serve a third term. He also founded the cities of Mobile and New Orleans. He never married and is buried in Paris, where he died in 1768.

William C. C. Claiborne was the first governor of Louisiana after statehood was granted in 1812. A native of Virginia, he was

Memorial Hall under construction, looking west toward the Senate chamber. Circle in the floor has been prepared for the large bronze seal.

appointed governor of the Mississippi Territory by President Thomas Jefferson and in 1805 was sent to administer the territory of Orleans. After serving as governor, he was elected to the United States Senate in 1817. His descendents still live in the Baton Rouge area.

Henry Watkins Allen was Louisiana's Confederate governor in 1864 and 1865. A member of the state legislature when the Civil War broke out, Allen enlisted in the Delta Rifles and was twice wounded in battle, at Shiloh and in the Battle of Baton Rouge. He was elected governor of Louisiana during the war and served in the temporary capitol at Shreveport. When the war was over, he went to Mexico and died there in 1866.

Another hero was Francis Tillou Nicholls, a native of Louisiana. He lost an arm and a foot in the fierce fighting of the Civil War. Elected governor twice, he led the state during the troubled Reconstruction days. Nicholls is particularly remembered for his stand against the Louisiana Lottery Company. He declared that he did not want his right hand to dishonor the left hand, which he had lost in battle, by signing an extension of the lottery company charter.

The frieze around the outside of the building is repeated in majestic Memorial Hall, but with slight changes. If one looks closely, bits of scenery not appearing in the outside frieze can be viewed separating the various panels.

In the center of the floor in Memorial Hall is a bronze map of Louisiana with symbols showing the major product of each area, circled by a list of the sixty-four parishes. (Louisiana is the only state with parishes rather than counties.) In creating the design, the parish names were placed on a wooden track by architect Solis Seiferth and replaced and relocated until they all fit. He had made a list of parishes in descending order, with the longest name, St. John the Baptist, in first place and the shortest, Winn, at the end. Note the difference in the size of some letters; for purposes of symmetry, some of the *O*'s, for instance, are wider than others. The railing was added later after the feet of so many tourists had begun to wear away the bronze. Occasionally tourists, especially schoolchildren, toss coins into the enclosure, giving it the appearance of a wishing well. The coins are removed periodically and given to a children's charity.

On the balcony above the elevators is a medallion depicting Governor Huey P. Long, the moving force behind the conception and construction of the building. Governor Long is depicted four

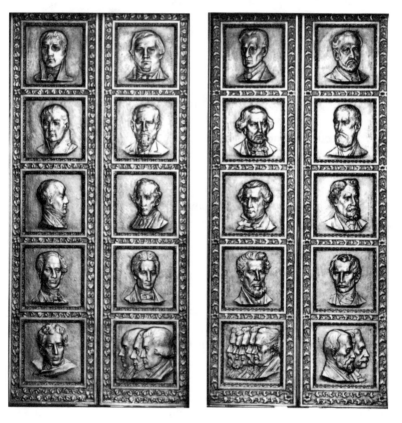

Bronze elevator doors in Memorial Hall bear the likenesses of Louisiana's governors from 1812 to 1932, when the capitol was dedicated. Note the architects' use of multiple portraits in three panels. Governor Huey Long occupies the honored position at the top right of the door on the right.

times in the capitol: here, on the elevator doors beneath the balcony, on the frieze outside the building, and in the similar frieze inside Memorial Hall.

Thirty-seven Louisiana governors grace the bronze elevator doors of Memorial Hall. When architect Seiferth was trying to decide what to do about the many governors of the Civil War and

Reconstruction periods, he asked Huey Long about omitting some of them. Long replied, quoting Montesquieu, "The truth of history is all or none." Seiferth proceeded to include all of them, even though it meant squeezing five portraits onto one panel.

On the elevator doors to the west, reading down, are:

Left	*Right*
William C. C. Claiborne, 1812-1816	Issac Johnson, 1846-1850
Jacques Phillipe Villere, 1816-1820	Alexandre Mouton, 1843-1846
Thomas Bolling Robertson, 1820-1824	Edward Douglass White, 1835-1839
Henry S. Johnson, 1824-1828	Andre Bienvenu Roman, 1831-1835, 1839-1843
Pierre Auguste C. B. Derbigny, 1828-1829	Henry Schuyler Thibodeaux, 1824; Jacques Dupre, 1830-31; Armand Beauvais, 1829-1830

On the center doors are:

Left	*Right*
Joseph Marshall Walker, 1850-1853	Samuel Douglas McEnery, 1884-1888
Paul Octave Hebert, 1853-1856	Louis Alfred Wiltz, 1880-1881
Robert Charles Wickliffe, 1856-1860	Francis Tillou Nicholls, 1877-1880, 1888-1892
Thomas Overton Moore, 1860-1864	Henry Watkins Allen, 1864-1865
Michael Hahn, 1864-1865; James M. Wells, 1865-1867; Benjamin F. Flanders, 1867-1868; Henry C. Warmoth, 1868-1872; Joshua Baker, 1868	John McEnery, 1872; William Pitt Kellogg, 1872-1876

On the doors to the east are:

Left	*Right*
Murphy James Foster, 1892-1900	Huey Pierce Long, 1928-1932
William Wright Heard, 1900-1904	Oramel Hinckley Simpson, 1926-1928
Newton Crain Blanchard, 1904-1908	Henry L. Fuqua, 1924-1926
Jared Young Sanders, 1908-1912	John M. Parker, 1920-1924
Luther Egbert Hall, 1912-1916	Ruffin G. Pleasant, 1916-1920

With the exception of a few, the governors are shown in chronological order, with those on the left-hand doors in ascending order and those on the right-hand doors in descending order. This design gave Governor Huey Long the preferred position at the extreme top right.

Both Roman and Nicholls served as governor twice, Roman having been out of office for four years and Nicholls for eight when reelected. Allen was the Confederate governor of Louisiana at the same time that Hahn governed for the Union. Warmoth and Kellogg were carpetbaggers. Pinchback's bust was added to Memorial Hall later; he does not appear on the doors because the legality of his brief term during Warmoth's impeachment proceedings is in question. John McEnery is shown because he was elected in 1872, although Kellogg was declared the winner by the Radical Returning Board. John McEnery was the brother of Samuel McEnery who took office in 1884.

Marble from every marble-producing country and every marble-producing state in the Union is included. Look about you as you walk through the first floor. The marble is particularly colorful and noteworthy in the Senate. The walls of Memorial Hall are of Levanto marble from Italy. The light green marble base is from Vermont, and the floor is Mount Vesuvius lava from Italy. The magnificent chandeliers above are so heavy they are anchored from an upper floor. The beautiful vases of Sevres porcelain and gold were given by France to Louisiana in 1934, two years after the capitol was completed. The plaques are written in French, a second language for many Louisianians.

P. B. S. Pinchback is depicted in a bust, added in 1976, at the west end of the chamber. Pinchback was the only black to serve as governor of any American state, having occupied the office for a month during Reconstruction. He did not serve the shortest term, however. Alvin O. King was governor for seventeen days, serving temporarily at the end of Huey's term when the latter finally resigned to accept his seat in the United States Senate.

A gold-leaf ceiling in a pattern of oak leaves lends a majestic touch to the great hall. It includes symbols of the Indians who

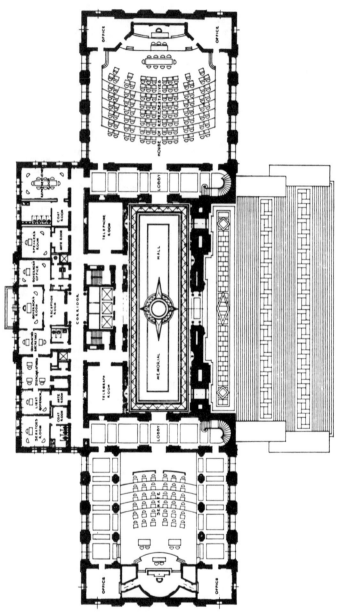

Architects' plan of the first floor of the capitol. Note the original layout of the north wing offices, which originally included the governor's office. It was in the corridor in front of the original governor's office that Huey Long was slain.

first lived in Louisiana, along with those of Spain, France, the Confederacy, and the United States. A time capsule commemorating the Bicentennial stands at the right outside of the door to the Senate, beneath the magnificent mural by Jules Guerin. Guerin, one of the most acclaimed artists to work on the capitol, came from France. He was in his late sixties when he completed this mural and its companion piece on the opposite end. The mural on the Senate end is called *Abundance of Earth* and depicts the Goddess of Agriculture. It is said that the artist could never again mix together the beautiful blue of the woman's garment in the lower right hand corner. The corresponding mural on the opposite wall over the entrance to the House of Representatives shows the Goddess of Knowledge.

The massive bronze doors in Memorial Hall and the legislative wings are among the most striking features of the capitol. Executed by the Piccirilli brothers of New York, they depict in lively and expressive fashion key scenes from Louisiana's history. The doors leading into the senate lobby from Memorial Hall depict, when closed, the following scenes (at **left**):

Discovery of the Mississippi River by Pineda (1519). Alonso de Pineda sailed along the Gulf Coast in 1519. He is shown here discovering the Mississippi River, although some scholars think he may have arrived at the Mobile River.

La Salle Visits the Kappas and the Arkansas (1682). A French fur trader based in Canada, La Salle explored the Lower Mississippi River Valley with an Italian, Henri de Tonti, in 1682 and a party that included thirteen Indian women and children. He reached the mouth of the river on April 7 and took possession of the country for France on April 9.(*Louisiane* means the "land of Louis.") Two years later the colony established by La Salle in Texas failed, and his own men killed him. This scene recreates his meeting with the Kappas and the Arkansas Indians.

Drowning of Narvaez at the Mouth of the Mississippi (1528). Panfilo de Narvaez landed in Florida in 1528, but after los-

Flags of Louisiana decorate the balcony overlooking the center of Memorial Hall. They represent (from right to left) Castile and Leon; Bourbon France; Bourbon Spain; England; France; United States (15 stars); Republic of West Florida; Louisiana

national flag; Confederate battle flag; Confederate Stars and Bars; Louisiana state flag; and the United States flag. A bronze likeness of Huey Long is beneath them.

ing many of his men in skirmishes with Indians, he continued to the Gulf of Mexico. Near the mouth of the Mississippi, his crude boats were wrecked, and the Spanish explorer drowned.

To the **right:**

Discovery of the Mississippi by De Soto (1541). The first panel delineates the arrival of Hernando De Soto at the Mississippi River.

Burial of De Soto in the Mississippi (1542). De Soto died somewhere in Arkansas, and was buried in the river. His gallant story is illustrated in the top two panels.

Iberville at the Mouth of the Mississippi (1699). Another Canadian, Pierre le Moyne, Sieur d'Iberville, who came to Louisiana in 1699, is shown at the mouth of the Mississippi River.

The discovery of the Mississippi by La Salle is portrayed in the space above the doors.

The reverse of these doors viewed from the Senate lobby shows the progress of the early explorers (at **left):**

Founding of Natchitoches by St. Denis (1714). Louis Juchereau de St. Denis came to Louisiana with Bienville and in 1714 was sent by Governor Antoine de le Mothe Cadillac to establish a post in north Louisiana. St. Denis founded Natchitoches on the Red River.

Bienville Meets the Ouaches and Bayougoulas at Bayou Plaquemines (1699). The Bayougoulas (Bayogoulas) were a fierce tribe, who later massacred their Quinipissa Indian brothers, but in this scene they are at peace. They were the ones who had saved the letter of Tonti since 1685.

Bienville Halts the English at English Turn (1699). The same year that Bienville was given the 14-year-old Tonti letter, he proceeded down the river below what is now New Orleans, rounded a bend in the Mississippi, and saw a British ship. Sailing to the ship, he informed the captain that the

British were in French territory and that a French fleet was up the river. The captain, Lewis Banks, believed the story and sailed away. This part of the stream is still called "English Turn" because of Bienville's successful ruse.

At the **right** are:

Founding of New Orleans by Bienville (1718). Bienville chose a crescent in the river as the site for New Orleans because the bend was believed safe from tidal waves and hurricanes.

Building of Fort Maurepas by Iberville (1700). In 1700 Iberville decided to build a fort on the Gulf Coast and chose a site in Biloxi Bay. Here he built Fort Maurepas.

Iberville at the Natchez Village (1700). Iberville also traveled up the river as far as Natchez (about ninety miles above Baton Rouge) and visited the Natchez villages in 1700.

The center doors into the Senate proper when closed show (at **left**):

Natchez Massacre (1727). The Indians revolted against the tyrannical commandant Chepart, and nearly three hundred people were killed by the Natchez tribe.

Lafreniere and the Patriots Arrested by O'Reilly (1769). Alejandro O'Reilly, an Irishman who had settled in Spain, was the next Spanish governor sent out in 1760. He arrested six patriots who had led the rebellion, and they were sentenced to death by hanging for treason. Since no hangman could be found, five of the men were shot by a firing squad. The sixth man had died in prison. The widow of one of these prisoners later married a Spanish officer.

Arrival of the Casket Girls at New Orleans (1728). Casket girls were sent from France in 1728 to wed the settlers. Before the wedding could be arranged, the young girls were cared for by the Ursuline nuns, who had arrived in Louisiana in 1727. The little caskets or traveling bags of the girls are plainly seen here. The girls were of excellent character, sent out by the Company of the Indies.

Famed sculptor Attillio Piccirilli nears completion of the statue of Henry Watkins Allen that now stands in Memorial Hall. The small statuette at right is the plaster model from which Piccirilli worked.

To the **right** are:

The Expulsion of Ulloa (1768). In 1762 Louisiana was given
to Spain by France, but the first Spanish Governor, Don
Antonio de Ulloa, did not arrive until 1766. Ulloa was not
really a ruler but a scholar who had founded scientific lab-
oratories in Europe. So unpopular did he prove to be and
so troubled were these times of Spanish domination, that
Ulloa was ordered to leave by the Superior Council and
sailed furtively away down the river.

Galvez Appeals to the Louisianians (1779). In this scene Galvez prepared to attack Baton Rouge. He appealed to the

*Closeup view of the panel depicting the capture of the Spanish
fort at Baton Rouge, 1810. Located in the center on the right
of the door leading from Memorial Hall to the House of
Representatives.*

Bronze door on chamber side of the Senate. Scenes at left (from top) are Bienville and the Black Code, Code Napoleon, and Law of the Indies. Shown at right (from top) are the drafting of the U.S. Constitution, preparation of Louisiana's civil code, and the Baton Rouge Convention of 1861.

people for help in defending the province against the British.

Arrival of the Acadians (1764). French Canadians from Acadia in Nova Scotia came to Louisiana as early as 1756, although the greatest migrations took place between 1765 and 1786. Refusing to obey certain British laws, the Acadians were expelled from Nova Scotia, and their lands were burned. The poem *Evangeline* by Henry Wadsworth Longfellow records their tragic story.

The reverse sides of these doors are described as viewed from the Senate side, since they are seldom opened. The panels detail the legal history of Louisiana, beginning at the **left**:

Bienville and the Black Code (1724). Bienville's code provided protection for the slaves, as well as prohibitions.

The Preparation of the Code Napoleon (1801-1803). This code of law is still in use in Louisiana today.

O'Reilly Introduces the Law of the Indies (1769). The Law of the Indies was the entire body of the legal system that Spain imposed upon its colonies outside of Europe. The same O'Reilly who executed the rebels introduced the code to Louisiana.

At the **right** are:

The Drafting of the Constitution of the United States. The Constitution was drawn up in 1787.

The Preparation of the Civil Code of Louisiana. This was largely the work of Edward Livingston, who represented Louisiana in Congress. The first civil code in the Louisiana Territory followed French and Spanish law, but a new civil code was composed in 1825. A code of criminal law was adopted in 1828.

The Convention of 1861 in Baton Rouge. In 1861, the secession convention was held at Baton Rouge, during which Louisiana decided to withdraw from the Union. An election earlier that year had revealed that twenty-nine parishes fa-

Reverse of Senate-Memorial Hall door, from chamber side, shows (left panel, from top) the founding of Natchitoches, Bienville meeting the Bayougoulas, and Bienville halting British at English Turn. At right (from top) are the founding of New Orleans, the construction of Fort Maurepas, and Iberville visiting the Natchez.

vored secession and nineteen favored remaining in the Union.

The doors into the House of Representatives lobby from Memorial Hall depict, when closed, the following historical events (at **left**):

Signing the Louisiana Purchase Treaty (1803). This document, which led to the creation of the modern state, now reposes in the Library of Congress.

The Battle of New Orleans 8th January (1815). Andrew Jackson, commanding Tennessee and Kentucky backwoodsmen, local citizens, and Lafitte's pirates, successfully defended the city of New Orleans against the British.

The American Flotilla Resists the British Advance (1814). A small fleet of American ships, headed by Lt. Thomas Ap Catesby Jones, held off the British for a time in Lake Borgne. Although Jones's men were defeated, the British lost 175 men. American losses totaled only 6.

At **right** are:

Andrew Jackson on the Battlefield at Chalmette (1815). General Jackson won the last battle of the war on the plains of Chalmette outside New Orleans.

Capture of the Spanish Fort at Baton Rouge (1810). American and British citizens banded together against Spain and captured the Spanish fort at Baton Rouge. The Free State of West Florida was then established, it but lasted only a few weeks before being taken over by the United States.

Jean Lafitte and the Baratarians. Here Lafitte is seen coming ashore with his pirate band.

The transfer of Louisiana from France to the United States is pictured above the doors. From the inside of the House lobby the doors reveal (at the **left**):

Arrival of First Steamboat (1812). The *New Orleans* steamed down the river from Pittsburgh and ushered in the steamboat era.

Outer door to Senate proper portrays (at left, from top) the Natchez Massacre, arrest of patriots by O'Reilly, and the arrival in New Orleans of the celebrated casket girls. At right (from top) are the expulsion of Ulloa, Galvez' appeal, and arrival of the Acadians.

Signing of the Treaty with the Caddo Indians (1835). Land was purchased by the state from the Caddo Indians in north Louisiana. Today one of the Louisiana parishes bears the name of the tribe.

New Orleans of 1850. By 1850 New Orleans had become a busy town, well-situated on the river and easily reached by steamboat and railroad. That year saw the transfer of the capitol from New Orleans to Baton Rouge.

At the **right**:

The Ponchartrain Railroad (1831). The state's first railroad connected New Orleans with its suburbs.

The Making of Sugar by De Bore (1794). The first to granulate sugar from Louisiana sugarcane was Etienne de Bore, who in so doing, contributed immeasurably to the state's economic development. The kettle he used is now displayed on the Louisiana State University campus in Baton Rouge.

Reception Given to Lafayette (1824). The great hero of the American Revolution visited French Louisiana, stopping along the way at the Pentagon Barracks.

The doors into the House chamber on the lobby side show scenes after the turn of the nineteenth century (at the **left**):

Battle of Berwick Bay (1863). The Confederates built earthworks near Morgan City on the bay, and these were held alternately by both Rebels and Yankees.

Passing the Mississippi River Forts Below New Orleans (1862). Flag Officer David G. Farragut and his fleet bombarded the fortifications and sailed past them, leading to the occupation of New Orleans on April 28 by General Benjamin F. Butler.

The Mississippi River Jetties (1875-1879). James B. Eads fashioned a system of jetties which deepened the river, making the progress of steamboats safer. A famous hydraulics engineer, he worked with iron-clads during the Civil War, invented a diving bell, and built a steel bridge over the Mississippi River at St. Louis. He staked his reputation and

The pattern of oak leaves on the gold leaf ceiling of Memorial Hall creates a splendid background for the massive chandelier.

personal fortune on deepening the channel and succeeded in making New Orleans accessible to ocean-going liners. Today, huge ocean-going vessels regularly sail upriver to the port of Baton Rouge.

At the **right**:

The Battle of Mansfield (1864). General Alfred Mouton was killed in this north Louisiana battle which the Confederates won at great cost in lives and materiel.

Battle of New Orleans for Freedom (1874). Postwar riots took place in the city during turbulent Reconstruction days.

Roosevelt's Visit to New Orleans (1905). President Theodore Roosevelt visited New Orleans in 1905. It was on a hunting trip in neighboring Mississippi that Roosevelt ordered a small bear released unharmed. The papers made much of his action, and the manufacture of Teddy Bears was launched.

On the chamber side, the House doors show the various capitols of Louisiana, not in chronological order (at the **left**):

The Cabildo, New Orleans (1812)
State House, Donaldsonville (1830)
State House, New Orleans (1832-1850)

At the **right**:

State House, Baton Rouge (1850-1932) Original Building Built and Reconstructed
War Time State House, Shreveport (1863-1865)
State House of the Reconstruction Era, St. Louis Hotel, New Orleans.

Of these, the Cabildo in New Orleans and the Old State Capitol in Baton Rouge are still standing.

The headdress of an Indian, one of the early inhabitants of Louisiana, is painted in the corner of the ceiling of Memorial Hall.

The bust of P. B. S. Pinchback, the only black governor of Louisiana, was added to Memorial Hall in 1975. Pinchback served as acting governor during an embattled period in 1873.

A carved marble Indian head, a somewhat rare reproduction, adorns a bench in Memorial Hall.

Memorial Hall vase, one of a pair donated by the French government in 1934. The vases were made in Sevres, a city near Paris famous for its porcelain.

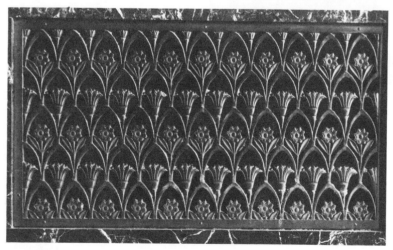

Grillwork on the main floor shows the meticulous attention to detail by the building's designers.

The bronze railing enclosing the map in the center of Memorial Hall bears this seal of Louisiana, a pelican feeding her young.

Detail of border of door from Memorial Hall to House of Representatives symbolizing transportation in Louisiana.

Detail of one of the columns in the capitol's back corridor near Memorial Hall carries reproductions of a turtle and an alligator, prolific residents of Louisiana's marshland. Huey Long was shot a few feet from this column.

*Office of the governor of Louisiana, located in the executive
suite on the fourth floor. Voting panel on the right enables the
governor to keep in touch with legislation during sessions of
the legislature.*

Governor's Office

Although the general public is not usually admitted to the governor's office, it deserves mention because of several items of interest. Pier glass mirrors from the Old State Capitol reflect the fourth floor reception room within their gold-leaf borders, and bronze busts from the Louisiana State Museum may be seen at the end of interior halls. The private office of the governor was formerly the Law Library, which has been moved to the twenty-fourth floor.

The former State Supreme Court Room is now used for press conferences. Here the visitor may see a mural painted by Conrad Albrizio which, appropriately enough, illustrates a passage from the *Bible*: "That judgment shall return unto righteousness and all the upright in heart shall follow it." The strong female figure of Justice is at the center of the mural, with the upright on one side and the children of darkness on the other. (Four more murals by Albrizio adorn the foyer of the State Capitol Annex across the street.) Symbols of harvest time grace the ornamental band that circles the room near the ceiling. Some of the original rows of chairs from the courtroom are still preserved here. The brass doors, decorated with pelicans, are similar to those that grace the governor's elevator.

The desk of the governor, fourth floor.

Waiting room, or "trophy room," adjacent to the governor's office, features mementoes of his career. At the extreme left are favorite political cartoons of the governor.

*Shining brass doors enclose
the governor's private elevator. The motif is the pelican,
Louisiana's state bird.*

*Portraits of noted Louisianians line this corridor of the gov-
ernor's suite.*

Reception area of the governor's office, on the fourth floor.

Governor's press room on the fourth floor was once the State Court of Appeals. Fresco mural by Conrad Albrizio in the background has been destroyed.

The governor conducts his press conferences from this speakers' stand in the old State Court of Appeals on the fourth floor.

Governor's office originally located off the rear corridor of the first floor. Note the electric fan, standard equipment in 1932, and the Art Deco-style light fixture.

A wide variety of marble is apparent in this striking view of the Senate.

Legislative Chambers—
The House and the Senate

The two legislative chambers occupy massive wings on each side of Memorial Hall. To the right is the House of Representatives; its original furniture of solid American walnut is still in use. The chandeliers are embellished with Louisiana birds at the top of the fixtures, and a frieze of Louisiana plants and animals may be seen near the ceiling. The tan and brown marbles show to advantage in the great spaces. Note that the natural-color stone is a volcanic lava formation.

The Louisiana state seal may be seen over the center doors. Louisiana is known as the Pelican State. The mother pelican is shown allegorically—feeding her young with her own blood as she pierces her breast with her beak. When the pelican was chosen as the state bird, the legislature failed to designate either the brown or the white pelican. In 1958 when the brown pelican was finally selected, it had almost disappeared from Louisiana, primarily because of the pollution of the waters. Attempts are being made to reintroduce the brown pelican into the state.

A portrait of the late U.S. Senator Allen J. Ellender, first Speaker of the House to preside in the new capitol building, hangs at the rear of the House chamber.

Both the Senate and the House have electric voting machines.

The tally can be seen in the governor's office as the votes are taken. On a visit to Baton Rouge humorist Will Rogers wrote a column about the state capitol, remarking that Huey Long ran the switchboard so it did not matter which buttons were pressed.

Rose marble is used in the Senate. The original furniture was replaced after the Senate chamber was bombed on April 27, 1970, apparently in connection with a local labor dispute. The bomb was planted near the Speaker's desk (the chamber was empty), but so strong was the building that comparatively little structural damage resulted. A splinter blasted into a back pillar at the east end of the balcony and a pen protruding from one of the hexagons on the ceiling can still be seen.

The Senate motif is comprised of stars. There are sixty-four stars in the ceiling and on the pillars to commemorate the sixty-four parishes of Louisiana. The wall of the Senate balcony is of

Artist's conception of the House of Representatives, prior to construction.

particular interest and worth a trip up the curving, floating stairs. A band across the top of the wall carries a design of oak trees and fish, with a line of stars above. Note the decorative bronze in the windows and the wall grilles. Pillars embellished with turtles, crabs, and crocodiles are in the back corridor connecting the two chambers. Solid brass doors can be found throughout the main floor.

Lobby outside the Senate chamber.

*Floating marble stairway of Fam-
oso Violet ascends to the Senate
gallery.*

*House of Representatives. Electric
voting panel on back wall is connected to another panel in the governor's office so the chief executive can observe voting. Stone walls
are banded with pilasters of Siens
Travertine marble. Unlike the Senate, the House has no columns.*

A view of the bronze doors leading into the House of Representatives. To the right is a portrait of Allen J. Ellender, first Speaker of the House to preside in the new capitol and later a United States Senator. Spectators' balcony is at top.

Center door inside House of Representatives reproduces earlier Louisiana capitols. At left (from top) are the Cabildo in New Orleans, State House in Donaldsonville, and State House in New Orleans; at right (from top) are State House in Baton Rouge, Civil War Capitol in Shreveport, and Reconstruction Period Capitol in the St. Louis Hotel in New Orleans.

View of the Senate from the spectators' gallery. Original furniture, designed by the architects, was replaced after a bomb exploded in 1970.

View of the Senate from floor level. Desks and chairs are of American walnut and laurel.

House of Representatives viewed from spectators' gallery.

Center entrance to Senate.

Stars band the pillars supporting the ceiling of the Senate.

A series of hexagons comprise the ceiling of the Senate chamber. Notice the motif of stars at connecting points: sixty-four in all, one for each Louisiana parish. Observant onlookers may see splinters and a ball point pen imbedded in the ceiling during a bomb explosion in the Senate chamber in 1970.

Stars decorate the Senate columns, and the Roman symbol of authority, the fasces (rods bound with axe), can be seen near the ceiling.

The wall separating the stairway from the Senate gallery is decorated with a graceful band of oaks and birds.

Bernardo de Gálvez

SPANISH GOVERNOR
OF
LOUISIANA
1776 - 1783

GÁLVEZ, WITH THE AID OF MILITIA AND VOLUNTEERS FROM
LOUISIANA, WON VICTORIES AT BATON ROUGE, MOBILE, AND
PENSACOLA DURING THE AMERICAN REVOLUTION. BY HIS DARING
LEADERSHIP HE DROVE THE BRITISH FROM THE
LOWER MISSISSIPPI VALLEY AND WEST FLORIDA, GIVING
SPAIN CLAIM TO THIS AREA AT THE CLOSE OF HOSTILITIES.
FOLLOWING THE TREATY WITH SPAIN IN 1819, THE ENTIRE
FLORIDA TERRITORY BECAME A PART OF THE UNITED STATES.

THIS TABLET WAS PLACED IN CELEBRATION OF THE
BICENTENNIAL OF THE AMERICAN REVOLUTION BY THE
LOUISIANA SOCIETY, DAUGHTERS OF THE AMERICAN
REVOLUTION, ON SEPTEMBER 21, 1975, WHICH DATE IS
THE 196TH ANNIVERSARY OF THE BATTLE OF BATON
ROUGE, FOUGHT DURING THE AMERICAN REVOLUTION.

Plaque honoring Bernardo de Galvez, Spanish governor from 1776 to 1783, commemorates the only battle fought in Louisiana during the Revolutionary War.

The brown pelican appears on numerous door knobs throughout the capitol in a reproduction of the state seal. Typically, ornithologists say, the mother pelican has a brood of three chicks, as depicted here.

Four-story-high allegorical figures dominate the base of the tower. Representing "the four dominating spirits of a free and enlightened people," they are Law (southwest corner), Science (southeast corner), Philosophy (northeast corner), and Art (northwest corner). Cherubs pose at their feet. The observation tower, to which access is gained through the large doorways near the top, offers a panoramic view of the Baton Rouge area.

The Tower

The top of the tower was meant to be not only physically but spiritually the crowning point of the building. The four tremendous figures by Ulric Ellerhusen at the twenty-second floor level represent Philosophy, Art, Law, and Science. These portray four dominant spirits of a free and enlightened people:

> *Law*, on the southwest corner, bears the familiar Roman symbol of authority, the fasces (a bundle of rods bound about an ax), and is a law that guides rather than punishes.
>
> *Science*, on the southeast corner, studies the problems of mankind, developing ways to "redeem man from the serfdom of arduous manual labor," in the words of the architect.
>
> *Art*, on the northwest corner, encompasses the beauty of life with a vase, a pen, and a scroll.
>
> *Philosophy*, forming the northeast corner, thoughtfully contemplates the problems of life.

All are winged, with cherubs at their feet; all are an integral part of the tower. Art historian Vincent Kubly has described them as part sculpture and part architecture. Exquisite motifs that can scarcely be seen from the ground below are used extravagantly

101

on the ornamental band at the base of the tower: sugarcane, crawfish, magnolia. All suggest Louisiana and its particular attractions.

To reach the top of the tower one takes the main elevator from Memorial Hall to the twenty-fourth level, transferring from the swifter, larger elevators to a smaller one where the building narrows. Note that the original controls are still in use in the small elevator. The area at the top is not aesthetically appealing, but it is interesting with its dioramas depicting the courtship of the wild turkey and a typical cypress swamp scene.

The observation tower offers a sweeping view of the area. To the west is ship traffic on the busy river. Here the Mississippi is at one of its widest points. Across the way are the lush cane fields of West Baton Rouge Parish and the little town of Port Allen, named after Governor Henry Watkins Allen. To the south one can see the new Mississippi River bridge and one of the many

Architects' plaster model of the base of the tower. Pelicans sit atop the four columns between each corner.

curves the river makes as it meanders toward the Gulf of Mexico. Note the busy port at the west bank.

Three miles to the south are the white oval roof of the Louisiana State University Assembly Center and the red tiles of campus buildings. The new upper deck of Tiger Stadium rises directly behind the Assembly Center. To the east, the stately white house on the lake is the Governor's Mansion, built in 1962, adjacent to the home of former governor Jimmie Davis. The brick-walled old Spanish Arsenal sits atop its knoll. Northward lies Exxon, the second largest oil refinery in the United States. (The largest is at Baytown, Texas.) The old bridge can be glimpsed beyond.

Detailed view of the Spirit of Law, on the southwest corner of the tower. Smiling cherubs flank fasces. Ulric Ellerhusen designed the four-story-high figures.

Inscribed over the four doors of the temple are Latin mottos, with an interesting correlation of *ad* and *vincit*:

Ad astra	To the stars
Vincit Omnia Veritas	Truth conquers all
Vincit Amor Patriae	Love of country conquers
Ad summum	To the heights

Massive eagle, one of four near the summit of the tower, with its creator, Lee Lawrie.

Ad astra formed part of a favorite axiom of senior architect Leon Weiss: *Per aspera ad astra*—"Through difficulties to the stars." It is carved on his tombstone.

The dominating spirits which rise four floors high are placed in relation to the mottos. Thus, Philosophy precedes "Truth conquers all"; Science is placed by the inscription, "To the stars"; Law comes before "Love of country conquers"; and Art proclaims, "To the summit." Towering above all is the great lantern symbolizing the light of Hope, Faith, Knowledge, and Truth.

Plaster model of tower. Lawrie eagle is near center.

The striking design of the capitol garden is evident in this view from the capitol tower. The statue of Huey Long is the center-piece of sunken garden design.

Capitol Grounds

The grounds surrounding the capitol, reflecting a historic past, are situated in the middle of Spanish Town where the early Spaniards settled. During the construction of the capitol, workmen accidentally uncovered numerous iron caskets containing the remains of many of these settlers, and they were reburied elsewhere.

Directly in front of the capitol in the sunken garden, where his funeral oration was delivered, stands a statue of Huey Long atop his grave. Executed by Charles Keck and erected in 1940, the massive bronze likeness faces the capitol Long created. At the base of the statue are bas reliefs of Long giving schoolbooks to children and exhorting the populace with upraised hand. "Share Our Wealth," Huey's credo and the name of a society he formed, is emblazoned across the front.

Inscribed on the statue is the following:

HUEY PIERCE LONG
1893-1935
GOVERNOR 1928-1932
UNITED STATES SENATOR
1932-1935

Here lies Louisiana's great son
Huey Pierce Long an unconquered
friend of the poor who dreamed of
the day when the wealth of the land
would be spread among all the people.
"I know the hearts of the people
because I have not colored my own.
I know when I am right in my own
conscience. I have one language.
Its simplicity gains pardon for
my lack of letters. Fear will not
change it. Persecution will not
change it. It cannot be changed
while people suffer."

HUEY PIERCE LONG
United States Senate
March 5, 1935

Erected by the state of Louisiana, 1940.

A cornerstone on Riverside Street to the west of the statue honors Zachary Taylor, U.S. Army general and twelfth president of the United States, known as "Old Rough and Ready" as a result of his exploits in the Mexican War. Taylor's house was located near this spot, and it was from his Baton Rouge home that he departed for Washington to assume the presidency. (He also owned a plantation in West Feliciana Parish. History records that he first learned of his nomination for the presidency when he walked down to the landing one day to greet steamboat passengers, who informed him he was the Whig party candidate.)

The red brick Pentagon Barracks, across the street to the southwest of the capitol, were built between 1819 and 1822. They were used as a garrison for federal troops from 1822 to 1877, except for a brief period when they were occupied by Confederates during the Civil War. When first constructed, the Pentagon served as the headquarters of the U.S. Army Southwest Command, which had responsibility for the western frontier. It also served as the base for American operations during the Mexican War, which led to Texas' independence. Many notable military figures served at the post, including Zachary Taylor, Robert E.

Lee, Ulysses S. Grant, William T. Sherman, George A. Custer, and Stonewall Jackson. Civilian visitors to the post included Henry Clay, Jefferson Davis, the Marquis de Lafayette, Vice-President John C. Calhoun, and presidents Abraham Lincoln, Warren G. Harding, and William H. Taft. From 1886 to 1925 the buildings were part of Louisiana State University, serving both

A 1932 view of the capitol garden, with early-day downtown Baton Rouge in the background. Dr. Carl Austin Weiss, accused of shooting Huey Long within the capitol, lived in a house two blocks from the left edge of the garden. The slender spire of St. Joseph Cathedral rises at top center.

as classrooms and dormitories until LSU moved to its present location in south Baton Rouge.

The Pentagon stands on the site of a British fort attacked in 1779 by Spanish forces led by Bernardo de Galvez. Galvez shelled the fort from an Indian mound located at the present-day corner of Convention and Lafayette streets, forcing the British to surrender. Only four of the projected five Pentagon buildings were ever constructed. The two buildings nearest the river housed enlisted men, while the other two served as officers' quarters for the original garrison. Ten 30-inch Doric columns distinguish each building on either side. Exterior walls were built thirty inches thick to withstand shelling.

Huey Long's statue stands before a background of modern downtown Baton Rouge.

The statue of General Claire Chennault, a native of Waterproof, Louisiana, and leader of the Flying Tigers of World War II, was donated by the Chinese government and erected near the Pentagon in 1976. The base is inscribed in English on the front and in Chinese on the back.

To the east of the capitol is the Old Spanish Arsenal, one of three powder magazines that originally served the post. Its four-foot-thick roof is sturdily supported by Spanish arches, and a brick wall surrounds it. The floor construction employs wooden pegs. It was built on a knoll, the highest point in the area. The arsenal now houses a museum, which contains a wide range of memorabilia related to Louisiana. Although renovated in 1962, the structure still reveals many historic features. Inscriptions carved by regiments occupying it during the Civil War can still be read on the inside wall to the right of the entrance.

The historic Pentagon Barracks, with the Mississippi River Bridge in the background. Such notable figures as Robert E. Lee, William T. Sherman, Zachary Taylor, George Custer, Stonewall Jackson, and Ulysses S. Grant served at the post. The Pentagon also was the site of Louisiana State University from 1886 until the move to its present site in 1925.

A replica of the Liberty Bell, cast in France to duplicate precisely in tone and structural detail the original bell, stands in front of the entrance. An Indian mound nearby is said to have yielded many artifacts some years ago.

The capitol grounds were landscaped by Edward Avery McIlhenny. He incorporated some of the original trees and bushes from the university campus and from the gardens of the home of Colonel Thomas D. Boyd, the last president of LSU on the site.

The Capitol Annex viewed from the west side of the capitol observation tower. Four murals by Conrad Albrizio decorate the lobby.

The Old Spanish Arsenal, east of the capitol, was constructed
on the highest point in the area. Once a powder magazine, it has
a four-foot-thick roof and an almost impregnable wall. Inscriptions carved by occupying soldiers during the Civil War can still
be seen on its inner walls. The building now houses a museum
with an excellent display of Louisiana memorabilia.

Iron caskets once containing the bodies of Spanish colonists
were unearthed during construction of the capitol. The capitol
stands in an area of Baton Rouge still known as Spanishtown.

Display in museum at Old Spanish Arsenal.

Display depicting Bernardo de Galvez, Spanish governor of Louisiana from 1776 to 1783, in the Old Spanish Arsenal museum.

Replica of the Liberty Bell stands outside the Old Spanish Arsenal. Cast in France, it duplicates the original Liberty Bell in both tone and structure.

Senator Huey P. Long was shot near the base of the column shown here, located in the north corridor of the capitol's first floor. The plaque on the wall marks the tragedy. Dr. Carl Austin Weiss allegedly waited for Long beside this column. Weiss' body, riddled with bullets from the guns of Long bodyguards, fell across the base of the column.

The Shooting of Huey Long

When Dr. Carl Austin Weiss stepped up to Huey Long in the back corridor of the capitol one September night in 1935, it was a meeting of two of the most brilliant but disparate men in south Louisiana. Dr. Weiss had graduated with a degree in medicine from Tulane University in 1927. After interning at Touro Infir-mary in New Orleans, he won a coveted internship at the American Hospital in Paris, on the recommendation of the famous Dr. Rudolph Matas. He studied in Vienna, attending lectures given in German; he planned to specialize in diseases of the ear, nose, and throat. In June, 1929, he began his work in Paris. En route home through New York, he inquired about opportunities at Bellevue Hospital and served there two years. In 1932 he returned to Baton Rouge to practice medicine with his father. In a short while, he married Yvonne Pavy of Opelousas, and some time later a son was born.

Dr. Weiss was many things that Huey Long was not: highly educated, reserved, deeply religious. He began that peaceful Sunday, September 8, by attending Mass and spent the rest of the lazy hours with his family. About nine o'clock that night he told his wife he had a call to make. She assumed he was going to the nearby Our Lady of the Lake Hospital. He lived only two blocks

117

Memorial plaque in honor of Huey Long, fatally wounded at this spot on September 8, 1935. The marks in the wall, believed by many to be bullet holes, actually are flaws in the marble.

from the capitol (the house has since been torn down), and his route could have taken him in front of the capitol.

There was a parking place in front of the capitol steps. Automobiles were not numerous in those days in the little city. Besides, many legislators stayed at "Huey's hotel"—the Heidelberg—and walked over from Lafayette Street to the state house. Weiss parked his car and entered the capitol.

Meanwhile, Huey walked down the back corridor behind Memorial Hall by himself, pulling away from the men who usually surrounded him. He went into the governor's office for a moment, and when he emerged, his bodyguards were there. It was not the custom of Louisiana politicians to have bodyguards. The son of Governor Henry L. Fuqua recalls that his father walked casually to work every day and that Fuqua often strolled

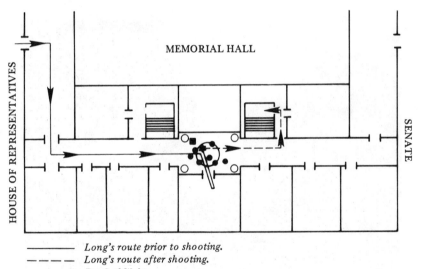

———————— Long's route prior to shooting.
— — — — Long's route after shooting.
■ Dr. Carl Weiss
✸ Huey Long
● Bodyguards and associates   Artwork by Julie Ruckstuhl

Re-creation of the setting of the fatal shooting of Huey Long. After he was shot, Long ran down the nearby stairs and was taken to Our Lady of the Lake Hospital nearby.

alone down Third Street to the Elks Club to meet friends later in the day. But Huey was afraid. He had made many enemies, and earlier had hired a former prizefighter for protection. That night his bodyguards attended him as he walked down the hall. The group was joined by State Supreme Court Justice John B. Fournet. Usually there were many people waiting to see Long. If his vindictiveness repelled some, his sheer dynamism and rough charm attracted many others.

Dr. Weiss stepped up from his post near a marble pillar, and at that point history becomes clouded. He may have spoken to Huey; he may have hit Long. (It was reported later in a notarized statement by a nurse at the hospital that Huey had a cut on his lip.) Murphy Roden, the bodyguard next to Long as he came into the corridor, testified that a young man in a white linen suit with

Dented wrist watch worn by Murphy Roden, Huey Long's bodyguard. Roden testified at an inquest that a bullet from the gun of Dr. Carl Austin Weiss was deflected by the watch case during the scuffle in which Long was fatally shot.

a hat in his hand stepped up and fired an automatic pistol at Huey. Roden later said a second bullet shattered his wrist watch, but at the coroner's inquest he stated only one shot was fired. Scuffling with Weiss, Roden slipped and fell on the marble floor.

The bodyguards began firing. Long, struck by a bullet, ran toward the stairs. The senator was rushed to the nearby Our Lady of the Lake Hospital, the same hospital Yvonne Weiss thought her husband had set out to visit. Weiss, however, was killed instantly in a storm of bullets loosed by the bodyguards.

Casket bearing the body of Huey Long is carried down the capitol steps by his close friends and political colleagues: (at left of casket, from front) Governor Oscar K. Allen, Lt. Governor James A. Noe, and (obscured behind Noe) Allen J. Ellender, Speaker of the House of Representatives; (at right of casket, from front) Seymour Weiss, Associate Justice of the State Supreme Court John B. Fournet, and Robert S. Maestri.

On the House floor, Sergeant-at-Arms Arthur J. "Tommy" Thomas heard that Huey had been shot and rushed to the telephone in his little office near the Speaker's desk. He called his family with the news, then dashed into the corridor, pushing his way through the crowd gathered there. He recognized the body at the foot of the pillar as his Fifth Street neighbor. "My God," he said, "it's Carl Weiss." At the hospital politicians crowded into the operating room. "I don't want anybody to issue any

The funeral of Huey Long in the capitol garden. A statue was later erected over his tomb.

statements or do any talking until I get out of here," Long announced firmly. "I'll issue all the statements."

Thirty hours later, Long died of internal hemorrhaging after an operation that failed to save his life. Doctors had come from all over the state to attend him. The *Times-Picayune* extra on September 9 announced (an unfounded rumor, it developed) that one of the famous Mayo brothers from Rochester, Minnesota, was on his way to Baton Rouge by plane and that "the Baton Rouge airport had been lighted."

At the inquest held eight days after the shooting—an inquest that was scheduled four times before the witnesses appeared—Justice John B. Fournet testified that he saw Weiss with a gun and tried to deflect it with his hat. One of the bodyguards asked to be excused from testifying, and permission was granted. Other witnesses in the corridor told similar stories of a man with a gun hidden behind his hat. The inquest was the only official investigation of the shooting.

In Baton Rouge to this day, natives say a stray bullet intended for Weiss and fired in the melee reached Huey. It was not unusual at the time for physicians to carry guns at night. And the bullet that penetrated Long was never produced, for it passed completely through the body.

Many questions about Long's death remain unanswered. Why did Dr. Weiss stop at the capitol? There was talk that Long had spread slanderous remarks about the Pavy family, but no one was ever able to prove that Long had done so, or that the family had heard them. Long was preparing to gerrymander Judge Benjamin Pavy, Weiss's father-in-law, out of office, but the family was apparently not upset since that would have given Judge Pavy more time for his family. A cousin of Weiss declared that when he went to the capitol later that night to check Weiss's car, the doctor's instrument bag had been rifled, as had the glove compartment. The keys were not in the car, and they were not turned over to the family. Yet the next day, when the cousin returned to the capitol, the car had been moved from its parking place.

Thus, two relatively young men—a political genius and a skilled physician—with much in life before them, died as a result of that meeting, a meeting marked by a simple plaque on the bullet-pocked wall:

Huey P. Long
United States Senator
and
Former Governor of Louisiana
Died September 10, 1935 From a Bullet
Wound Inflicted Here on September 8, 1935
He Was 42 Years Old

Statue of Huey Long obscures the capitol he conceived and caused to be built.

Index

125